The Snark Handbook
Clichés Edition

Also by Lawrence Dorfman

The Snark Handbook:
A Reference Guide to Verbal Sparring

The Snark Handbook: Insult Edition:
Comebacks, Taunts, Retorts, and Affronteries

The Snark Handbook: Sex Edition:
Innuendo, Irony, and Ill-Advised Insults on Intimacy

Snark! The Herald Angels Sing:
Sarcasm, Bitterness, and the Holiday Season

The Snark Handbook: Politics & Government Edition:
Gridlock, Red Tape, and Other Insults to We the People

The Cigar Lover's Compendium

The Snark Handbook
Clichés Edition

OVERUSED BUZZWORDS, HACKNEYED PHRASES, AND OTHER MISUSES OF THE ENGLISH LANGUAGE

LAWRENCE DORFMAN

In collaboration with James Michael Naccarato

Skyhorse Publishing

Skyhorse Publishing books may be purchased in bulk at special discounts for sales promotion, corporate gifts, fund-raising, or educational purposes. Special editions can also be created to specifications. For details, contact the Special Sales Department, Skyhorse Publishing, 307 West 36th Street, 11th Floor, New York, NY 10018 or info@skyhorsepublishing.com.

Skyhorse® and Skyhorse Publishing® are registered trademarks of Skyhorse Publishing, Inc.®, a Delaware corporation.

Visit our website at www.skyhorsepublishing.com.

10 9 8 7 6 5 4 3 2 1

Library of Congress Cataloging-in-Publication Data is available on file.
ISBN: 978-1-61608-635-0

Printed in China

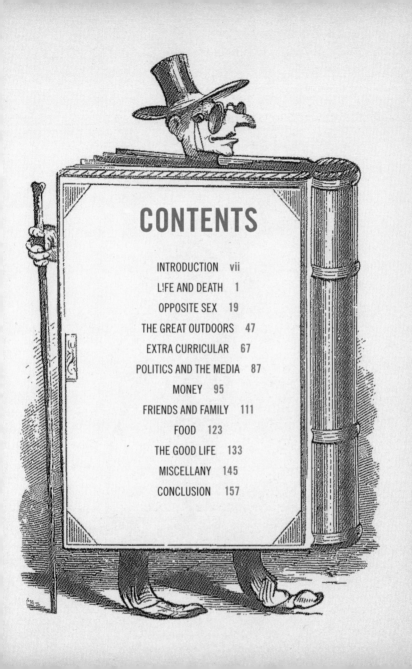

CONTENTS

Introduction

"Last, but not least, avoid clichés like the plague."
—WILLIAM SAFIRE

CLICHÉ : NOUN
    Etymology: French, literally, printer's stereotype, from past participle of cliché r to stereotype, of imitative origin

    Date: 1892

    1 : a trite phrase or expression; also : the idea expressed by it
    2 : a hackneyed theme, characterization, or situation
    3 : something that has become overly familiar or commonplace
    4: Overused

I detest cliché's with a passion. In the words of Stephen Frye, "It is a cliché that most clichés are true, but then like most clichés, that cliché is untrue."

Clichés are like rationalizations.* Try going a week without using one . . . can't be done.

They are the hobgoblin of little minds. For many, they are the drug of choice. For most of us, once you begin to take notice, they are fingernails on a blackboard.

From Shakespeare (the undisputed King of the cliché) to Shakira; in music, on television, at the movies . . . in the boardroom, on a conference call, online or in person (offline?), clichés have overtaken the world.

And while some might say they're just misunderstood, they didn't start out that way. There was a time when they were new and vibrant. Once, they were clever and pithy. Now, they're just predictable. They're a way to say something when there's a pause in the conversation. Some think it's better than the popular use of the words "like" and "you know" . . . not a chance. Both affectations are annoying. The fall-back cliché is

---

* TAIC - Trite and Inane Cliché

just that . . . something to "fall back" on when your brain shuts down, your sense of humor is on vacation, and your tongue is fast asleep. Resist. You'll be better for it.

This book is a collection of many of the most overused ones. And after each one, a snark. A snide remark to point out to the user how trite he/she sounds.

Hopefully, it'll make you laugh. Hopefully, it'll make you think.

But, at the end of the day, the early bird catches the worm and slow and steady wins the race . . .

Kill me now.*

* TAIC

The Snark Handbook
Clichés Edition

Life and Death

"I feel like a cliché."
—JONATHAN CARROLL

WHEN THE GOING GETS rough, people tend to fall back on the lifelines that cliché's have become for them today. In this chapter, as we delve into Life and Death, Heaven and Hell, Good and Evil, Blood, Sweat, Tears . . . one can see where the quick fix of a fallback cliché might be a hardy temptation . . . resist it . . . you'll thank me later.

"The first man to compare the cheeks of a young woman to a rose was obviously a poet; the first to repeat it was possibly an idiot."

—SALVADORE DALI

Close only counts in horseshoes

+

Cope with grief

+

Years young

+

Don't fly off the handle

+

Everything's copasetic

+

Final good-byes

+

God help us

+

Existential angst

+

Moment of glory

+

Twilight years

+

Up the creek

+

What comes around, goes around

+

Life and limb

+

Spring to life

+

Take it easy

+

Take the plunge

+

These things happen

+

Trials and tribulations

+

Shallow grave

+

RESIDENTS + CLOUDLESS SKY + FAR CRY + GROU

Bite the dust / Bite your lip /
Bite the bullet / Bite your tongue—come on, bite
something already, anything.

◆◆

Blood is thicker than water—and a lot harder to get
out of clothing.

◆◆◆

Time heals all wounds—Bullshit. Drugs heal all
wounds. Time does nothing except go by.

◆◆

Blood money—Always welcome at many of your finer
establishments . . . otherwise Vegas would still be a
desert.

◆◆◆

You've got blood on your hands—**Don't say anything until you see a lawyer.**

++

I spent my blood, sweat, and tears—**and all I ever get is some schmuck singing about a dumbass spinning wheel.**

+++

Ashes to ashes, dust to dust—**not to mention a few bone fragments, a ligament or two . . . all things visceral, Sherlock.**

++

You're gonna be dead meat—**but given the choice, that's a whole lot better than being a dead vegetable, no? I mean, wouldn't you much rather be a hearty steak than a limp and flaccid broccoli?**

+++

The only thing certain are death and taxes—and Congress keeps trying to find ways to tax you long after you've died.

++

He's gone, but not forgotten—Well . . . not yet. Give it a few days. It's like swallowing a cherry stone . . . it'll pass.

+++

You can't take it with you—so I'm definitely going to spend every last dime I have before I go.

++

What a way to go—As if there's a choice? I'll just wait for the next "death" to come around if you don't mind.

+++

You only live once—Not necessarily, Mr. Bond.

++

He was talking into his hat—Right . . . and we have to live with it after he puts it back on his head and walks away scott free.

+++

You throw filth on the living and flowers on the dead— Always good to see a man with priorities.

++

He's bad to the bone—but always ready to party.

+++

See no evil, hear no evil, speak no evil—Curious, nobody said a thing about "Do No Evil." Must be okay. Go to town.

++

I'm in seventh heaven—Shootin' a little high there, Sparky . . . settle for the first or the second heaven. Lower expectations will curb some of the disappointment.

+++

It's as hot as hell—What did you expect, the air conditioned wing? Move over Rasputin, and get a sweater.

++

Like a bat out of hell—Must be some kinda baseball team, not just over the fence, but clear out of hell. Impressive.

+++

Between the devil and the deep blue sea—what are you talking about here, a friggin' surfboard? Hang ten? That can't be right . . . Hangin' cloven hooves? Bingo. Gnarly, Luci baby.

++

I catch hell if I do, and catch hell if I don't—so the hell with it, here comes your catcher.

+++

I'm going to hell in a hand basket—
Personally, I was hoping for a limo. Not a lot of room in a hand basket and I'm definitely bringin' a few folks with me.

++

The Devil must be beating his wife—Not likely. We ALL know who wears the horns in that household.

+++

Actions speak louder than words—To paraphrase Woody Allen, I never met anyone who didn't understand a slap in the face or a slug from a .45.

++

All's fair in love and war — but most times you can't tell
the two apart.

+++

You only hurt the one you love — and that's because
nobody else gives a shit what you do or would even put
up with what you do.

++

It's better to have loved and lost than never to have
loved at all — Nah, not buyin' it, not one lil' bit.

+++

Absence makes the heart grow fonder — Is it really
the heart? Pretty sure absence makes the . . . hell, I
don't know, can't remember now . . . maybe it was
"abstinence" . . . what does abstinence make grow
again?

++

Is the Pope Catholic?—Yeah, yeah . . . and the bear shits in woods and a chicken has lips . . . although, some Vatican watchers may actually question that first one.

+++

You're off your rocker—Whew! Vince Neil must be breathing easier.

++

You must be out of your mind—Clearly . . . and leaving my body on auto pilot. See you on the ground.

+++

He's as neat as a pin—Some might whisper OCD. Just sayin'.

++

Better the devil you know than the devil you don't—
Actually, I'll stick with the devil I don't know and never
have to meet.

+++

He bought the farm—and this is an expression for
dying? Old MacDonald had a farm and then a massive
coronary and "bought the farm." Nice.

++

Fools rush in where angels fear to tread—Always make
it a practice to follow the fearless angels. They'll catch
most of the flack.

+++

There's a sucker born every minute—and it looks like
today is pretty much everybody's birthday.

++

Ask me no questions and I'll tell you no lies—Huh? So what, you want me to ask you questions, then? 'Cos, the way you phrased that, it's fairly convoluted.

+++

Wisdom is not truth—Yeah, but then again, truth is pretty much open for debate.

++

You're driving me insane—It's kind of a short drive. The gas meter didn't move at all.

+++

Always look out for number one—Although number two can really be a killer worth watching out for, too. Had to have that second bean burrito, right?

++

I've got my back against the wall—Luckily, I have a
blindfold in my pocket.

✦✦✦

Mind your manners—Or is it man your minors . . .
make fun of mourners . . . something like that.

✦✦

He's all eyes and ears—He may be all eyes but I'm
having a whole lot of trouble getting past those ears,
Dumbo.

✦✦✦

All is vanity—Who you kidding? You're vain. ALL
is a laundry detergent. Therefore, you're a laundry
detergent. Makes sense, no?

✦✦

He went through the roof—Sort of solved our problem . . . Elvis left the building, too.

+++

You have to turn the other cheek—What . . . and get that one slapped too? Okay, c'mon, I'm a man, I can take it. Hey!! Not so hard.

++

You need to read the handwriting on the wall—With your luck, they'll end up being gang tags and you'll end up getting your ass kicked.

+++

What a way to go—Actually, does it even matter? It all pretty much ends up the same, anyway . . . and you're dead a long time.

++

Name your poison—Does anyone ever get that? Yeah, let's see . . . I think I'll go with cyanide, because arsenic always gives me a nasty heartburn.

+++

Make it down and dirty—Despite paying $10,000 for a coffin, it's the way we're all going to end up. Down and dirty. No other way TO make it.

++

She could be her evil twin—and really, how will you ever tell them apart?

+++

The Devil must be beating his wife—Hey, her parents warned her he was no good. Some kids never listen. You'd have thought the horns, tail, and all that fire would have given it away.

++

Don't look back, the Devil might be gaining—Doesn't really matter if you look back or not, he's pretty much got this race all sewn up.

+++

It's as easy as 1-2-3—Don't overestimate yourself, Einstein . . . these days, that's just beta testing.

++

He's on an emotional roller coaster—More like emotional bumper cars, careening from one crash to the next. Should have worn a helmet.

+++

To be honest/To tell you the truth—So what . . . everything beforehand has been a lie? Or is it that you usually lie your ass off.

++

Cliché Hall of Famer #1 - Ben Franklin*

"Beer is living proof that God loves us and wants us to be happy."

"Little boats should keep near shore"

"He that goes a borrowing goes a sorrowing."

"Those things that hurt, instruct."

"Men forget but never forgive. Women forgive but never forget."

"Originality is the art of concealing your sources"

"Life's tragedy is that we get old too soon and wise too late"

---

* Guess all that electricity flowing through his veins didn't stop the cliché thing.

Opposite Sex

"Forever poised between the cliché and the
indiscretion."
—HAROLD MACMILLAN

WHEN IT COMES TO the opposite sex, relying
on a cliché can either help your cause immensely . . .
or cause you to suffer from a slow and painful death.
The key lies in one's ability to take somethign trite and
make it one's own. Nearly impossible to do. Hasn't
stopped anyone from trying, though.

> "You need clichés. Clichés are what people respond to."
> —MATTHEW VAUGHN

Cat-like grace

It changed his/her life forever

Doesn't know if she's washing or hanging out

A faint heart never a true love knows

Got knocked up

Hanky panky

To your heart's content

Went storming off in a huff

Twist of fate

Fashion victim

Don't upset the apple cart

Don't get your knickers in a twist (English)

Don't trust the lock to which everyone has a key

Give and take

He/she is as dense as a London fog

Meaningful relationship

We're at loggerheads

Significant other

It's like I'm talking to a brick wall—One that really needs repointing . . . and I get better answers from the wall.

+++

She's as beautiful as the day is long—Just remember . . . the day always ends with night . . . dark, terrifying, ugly night. And that can be mighty long, too.

++

It's as plain as the nose on your face—Sorry kiddo, in your case, it's as plain as the face beneath your nose.

+++

Beauty is in the eye of the beholder—but just wait until the beholder gets glasses.

++

They say beauty is only skin deep—Well, if it wasn't, plastic surgeons would be much richer and dermatologists would rule the world.

+++

He's as big as a house—Yeah, and he's been packed on an addition to the kitchen and an in-law apartment to boot.

++

You make a better door than a window—Hey, I've always been more of a door man—check out those knockers.

+++

She fell out of the ugly tree and hit every branch on the way down—Clearly, she likes climbing back up there, over and over and over.

++

Beauty is a fading flower—The more plastic there is and the more artificial it be, the better.

+++

She likes 'em tall, dark and handsome—But short, pale, ugly, and obscenely rich pretty much trumps those emotions every time.

++

She's not the only fish in the sea—As if I was looking for someone who lack limbs with digits.

+++

Shotgun wedding—No worries. As long as I can throw my Best Man in front of me, I'm good to go.

++

Your place or mine?—Mine has the whipped cream,
the feathers, the whips, the harness ... what's that?
Yours? Well, okay, if we have to.

+++

He's got ants in his pants—I swear she said she was just
adjusting my underwear, although my uncle is royally
pissed.

++

Wanna play "Hide the salami?"—That's a lot of big talk
... seems more like "Wanna hide the Kosher minis?"
Does this Deli thing work for you much?

+++

You wash my back, I'll wash yours—Drop the soap
once and this party's over, Coach.

++

They were making the beast with two backs—What a lovely image . . . so biblical. Sex was so unimaginative back then.

+++

She's tugging on your chain—Uh, sure, that's my chain alright . . . You just keep tuggin'. I'll let you know when to stop . . . actually, you'll know when to stop.

++

He must be pulling your leg—Make up your mind, leg or chain. You really need an anatomy class.

+++

If you love something, set it free—Okay, fine . . . be like that. Know anybody that wants to buy a pair of handcuffs, only slightly used?

++

She's hot to trot—Man, don't you just love those animal euphimisms? And here I am, only prepared for a footrace. Maybe I can find a trotter somewhere.

+++

A spoon full of sugar helps the medicine go down— Life rule: Beware of anyone quoting from Mary Poppins. Besides, it's only good advice where oral sex is concerned. Mints or Lifesavers work, too.

++

I'm back in the saddle—I love it when you talk equestrian to me . . . I keep getting all these fabulous images when you say that. Can you whinny?

+++

A good man is hard to find—Or is it a hard man is good to find? Either way, you're screwed.

++

CREEK ✦ HUSHED COURTROOM ✦ TOOK A STEP TOWARD

Cold hands, warm heart—Fine, just keep them above the waist and away from my genitals.

+++

Cry me a river—So I can get into a boat and paddle away from you as quickly as possible.

++

Eat, drink, and be merry—I'll be Merry, you be Frank. God, I love this whole cross-dressing thing.

++

He's always blowing his own horn—That is one flexible double-jointed son of a bitch.

+++

He's as stiff as a board—Be fun to call on him to stand and answer questions, no?

++

His left hand doesn't know what his right hand is doing—Come to think of it, nobody actually wants to know what his right hand is doing.

+++

Love thy neighbor—Saves on travel, hotel rooms, phone bills . . .

++

I wouldn't kick her(him) outta bed for eatin' crackers— Why not? Ever lay in wet crackers? Not pleasant at all, let me tell. Saltines? Absolute worst.

+++

You can tell the men from the boys by the price of their toys—Don't you just love that men have to take their toys out to dinner before they get to play with them?

++

You can never be too rich or too blonde—Not really true . . . you can be too blonde. They need to be able to see you when you're laying on the beach. Those sand sweepers can leave a nasty mark.

♦♦♦

She wears her heart on her sleeve—It's either time for a new bra or a serious diet, babe.

♦♦

What you see is what you get—Note to self: Make sure you're out of there before she takes off the makeup.

♦♦♦

Altitude is determined by attitude—Never really understood this one. Does that mean you need to be high to get high? Or are you saying you can't get up unless you do a mood adjustment . . . Might we get a little clarity here, Sport?

♦♦

Always look on the bright side—Okay, maybe . . . but the Dark side is so much easier and, more often than not, sexier. At the very least, can I wear sunglasses?

+++

He's got an enormous chip on his shoulder— Something tells met this isn't about a football injury . . . or cookies . . . Or potatoes?

++

I was choked with emotion—That wasn't emotion, Hoss . . . that was like the rest of us, getting sick to our stomachs.

+++

Don't make me do something I'll regret—Oh, go ahead . . . a little regret is good for the soul . . . like, I regret talking to you . . . but of course, now that I have, I can always just blame it on you.

++

Smile and the world smiles with you, cry and you cry alone—Yes, but throw a temper tantrum and you'll have everybody's attention. Might just get something to cry about, my friend.

◆◆◆

That was a blast from the past—Really? Funny, my past sort of oozes toward me, wrapping sticky tendrils around my ankles and dragging me back to some primordial ooze where I have to account for all my sins. Yikes . . . sorry, didn't know all that was going to come out.

◆◆

Always a bridesmaid—That should be telling you something.

◆◆◆

Beat around the bush—Drunken first sexual encounter or some retro political campaign slogan? Your guess.

◆◆

Colder than a witch's tit in a brass bra—On sale now from the Victoria's Secret Witch's Tit Collection.

+++

Don't tempt fate—Because fate, what she really likes, is to be caressed ever so slightly just under her left breast while you whisper clichés in her right ear.

++

Don't let the bedbugs bite—Change hotels, ya moron.

+++

Everything's coming up daisies—I hate that. I start talking about nuclear arms and she ALWAYS changes the subject to daisies. Daisies?

++

Flattery will get you nowhere—No? It certainly seems to be working for me at the bar every Friday night.

+++

He's thinking with the wrong head—like we have a choice. It's part of our DNA.

++

Hey, just putting it out there—Well, just put it back in there, asswipe.

+++

I woke up at the crack of dawn—and boy, was she not happy about it.

++

I'm as happy as a clam—just waiting to be sucked out by some pretty mouth.

✦✦✦

Is that a gun/mouse/banana in your pocket or are you just happy to see me?—God, I really wish it were a gun.

✦✦

Patience is a virtue—but virtue gets you absolutely nothing in today's market. Sluttiness, on the other hand . . . that's got real value.

✦✦✦

To each his own—Used to think it was "To Eat his Own," but soon realized that was not actually possible without spinal surgery.

✦✦

You couldn't hit the broad side of a barn—**since when
did barns become gender specific?**

+++

Life's a bitch—then you die . . . or get married.

++

All dressed up and nowhere to go—Yeah, but if you
were naked, your dancecard would be completely
filled up.

+++

I was blown away—Hey, away . . . at home . . . it's all
good.

++

She a beautiful blushing bride—and he's a very nervous best man . . . coincidence? I think not.

+++

I have a bone of contention to pick with you—Don't you just hate it when men have pet names for their genitals . . . and what kind of name is "contention" anyway?

++

Bottoms up—Ah, yes, brings me right back to my prison days.

+++

Boys will be boys—With transgender the hot new thing, that's not exactly a truism these days.

++

Brand spankin' new—Whole new *50 Shades of Grey* meaning these days.

+++

As far as the eye can see—Used to be as far as the naked eye could see, but so many people are so incredibly myopic these days, they can only see as far as the closest mirror.

++

Be there or be square—Typically muttered by THE most unhip person in the room . . . .

+++

As plain as the nose on your face—or, in your case, as plain as the face beneath your nose.

++

She has a green thumb—Unfortunately, it's usually stuck quite far up her ass.

+++

Let's blow this pop stand/joint—Everything always ends up being about oral with you, doesn't it?

++

I was blown away—See above. I rest my case.

+++

They're getting hitched—How interesting . . . one little adverb and you've added an S&M take to this thing.

++

Gotta teach 'em about the birds and the bees—Huh.
Even though they've been watching people do it on
Cinemax for years, you're still sticking to the whole
nature analogy?

+++

There's something I've been meaning to tell you—Not
exactly what you want to hear as you notice the very
large Adam's apple on the girl you just took back to
your room.

++

It's all very tongue-in-cheek—Now that we have the
location down for that particular part of your anatomy,
how about we discuss where we should put those lips.

+++

She's very touchy-feely—Who doesn't love these little
sex expressions . . . until touchy-feelie starts to get all
"hot and bothered" and then watch "feely" get much
touchier.

++

He's got staying power—Ah yes, better living through chemistry, all in the magic of a little blue pill.

+++

Hope she comes a'callin—Doesn't usually happen so fast for me from just a'callin', Lil' Abner . . . I typically think about baseball. Pete Rose, specifically.

++

Come again?—Look at you, all demanding . . . wait until I finish this cigarette, 'kay?

+++

She's really the girl next door—Yeah, if you live in Amityville.

++

How do I love thee?—I could count the ways but I think I'll just refer to pages 17, 23, 102, and 103 of the Kama Sutra.

+++

Hey, whatever turns you on—What am I, a faucet? You could try doing some research occasionally, eh Kinsey? Maybe I should write a book . . .

++

What's going down?—Love the use of the "what," right? Not "who" . . . . Well, you almost got my attention.

+++

Doing the wild mambo—Aptly named from a dance with no steps . . . cuts way down on performance anxiety.

++

She's as flat as a board—We're talking personality, demeanor, affect, right? . . . oh yeah, and other things, too.

+++

It was a Freudian slip—Heard he liked to wear them under his tweeds, not to mention his Jungian panties and Heidegger push-up bra.

++

All things grow with love—Love? Okay, sure, we can call it that if it makes you happy.

+++

Give back tit for tat—I don't know, it must be awfully good "tat." Sounds like you're getting the better part of this deal.

++

Sweet 16 and never been kissed—she did say
"kissed," yes?

◆◆◆

To be honest/ to tell you the truth—So, what?
Everything beforehand has been a lie?

◆◆

Great Moments in Clichés - Authors

"Albatross around your neck"

–Samuel Taylor Coleridge

"Our greatest glory is not in never falling but in rising every time we fall."

–Confucius

"The camera makes everyone a tourist in other people's reality, and eventually in one's own."

–Susan Sontag

"It is not only what we do, but also what we do not do, for which we are accountable."

–Moliere

"What's done is done."

–William Shakespeare

"There is no way to prosperity, prosperity is the way."

–Wayne Dyer

"Don't go through life, grow through life."

–Eric Butterworth

"Not all those who wander are lost."

–J.R.R. Tolkien

"Never give in, never give in, never; never; never; never - in nothing, great or small, large or petty - never give in except to convictions of honor and good sense"

–Winston Churchill

"If you don't like something, change it. If you can't change it, change your attitude. Don't complain."

–Maya Angelou

"We are masters of the unsaid words, but slaves of those we let slip out"

–Winston Churchill

The Great Outdoors

"Adapt or perish, now as ever, is nature's inexorable
imperative."
—H. G. WELLS

AH, NATURE . . . The Great Outdoors. Big Sky
Country. God's Country. All God's Creatures,
Big and Small.
C'mon . . . stop already. We get it. Yes, there's
always been that innate need to be more well-spoken
when faced with the grandiose vista outside your
house. See the Wells quote above. My advice? Still the
same . . . resist . . . by all means.*

*TAIC

"Our writers are full of clichés just as old barns are full of bats. There is obviously no rule about this, except that anything that you suspect of being a cliché undoubtedly is one and had better be removed."

—WOLCOTT GIBBS

A green thumb

A nice day for a picnic

Barking up the wrong tree

You can't learn to swim without getting in the water

Taking the scenic route

Tell your story walking

A cloudless sky

Dog days

Weather the storm

You must row with the oars that you have

Early-morning hours

Many moons

Yer all wet

Fun in the sun

When life gives you lemons, make lemonade—or open a stand. Do SOMETHING. Life is clearly thirsty. Not real big on taking the subtle hints, are ya Sparky?

+++

When life gives you lemons—shut the fuck up. It could easily give you broccoli. You want broccoli? Yeah, that's what I thought . . .

++

An apple never falls far from the tree—and isn't it amazing how many bad apples one tree can produce?

+++

Apple of my eye—but a pain in my ass.

++

You're beating a dead horse—but it still pisses off
PETA.

+++

A bird in the hand is worth two in the bush—but a
bush in the hand is typically anywhere from
$50 to $100.

++

She's as blind as a bat—But hey, that's what you get
from sleeping upside down.

+++

It's a one-horse town—and they just handed me the
shovel.

++

That'll happen when pigs fly—Hey, I've been stuck on many an airline trip where I could have sworn . . .

+++

You can't teach an old dog new tricks—Nah, he'll just piss on the rug and hump your leg like always.

++

When you lie down with lions, you wake up with fleas—Sorry, not going to happen, any lying down will be the last thing you do . . . but look on the bright side, the lions won't have to eat for another few days.

+++

Naked as a jaybird—Right, because all the other birds are so dressed to the nines—what the hell does that cliché mean, anyway?

++

Once bitten, twice shy—Except if you're one of those Animal Planet hosts—then once bitten means higher ratings and a second season renewal.

+++

Waiting with baited breath—Because I'm what? A fish? Try some Listerine or Scope maybe . . . extra-strength with bait-removing particles . . .

++

The world is not my oyster—Nor is it any other kind of bivalve.

+++

You're barking up the wrong tree—Right, because dog behavior is so scientifically calculated . . . want to buy a picture of Einstein licking himself?

++

FIGURE　•　FIRESTORM/STORM OF PROTEST/CONTROVERSY

If you build a better mousetrap, the world will beat a path to your door—dropping off every friggin' mouse they can find.

+++

It shines like a diamond in a goat's ass—Tell me, just how do you know exactly how shiny that is? (And where did this cliché come from?)

++

Lie down with dogs and wake up with fleas—The alternative being lying down with pussies and getting crabs?

+++

His bark is worse than the bite—Really? Given how much of a jerk-off he is, that must be some frickin' bark.

++

It's like the blind leading the blind—A reminder to never buy a "slightly used" seeing eye dog that's advertised as "having great hearing."

+++

Birds of a feather flock together—Birds of different feathers end up on ladies' hats or as integral parts of sex toys.

++

He's the cat's pajamas—Yes, with an open flap in the back so he can lick himself.

+++

We were crammed in like sardines—Thankfully, we were able to coat ourselves in a really high-grade olive oil.

++

Even a blind squirrel finds an acorn sometimes—
More often than not, he finds the bottom of a set of
Michelin radials first.

✦✦✦

When the lion is dead, the hare jumps on his back—
Making all those "play dead" lessons pay off pretty
good for the lions, no?

✦✦

You can't make a silk purse out of a sow's ear—Hey,
give it time. I hear Bloomies is selling Sow's Ear purses
for serious bucks.

✦✦✦

A rose by any other name would smell as sweet—I guess
you can call them what you want . . . but I guarantee
that sending your wife a dozen American Beauty long
stemmed "spider warts" will not get you laid.

✦✦

Make like a tree and leave—I've been in like, a million forests, and I've never once seen a tree up and walk away . . . so what exactly are you talking about?

+++

As clear as mud. As cold as ice. As common as dirt. As delicate as a flower. As pure as snow.—Okay, I get it, Captain Obvious. How about as pointless as this stupid cliché?

++

She's as cold as ice—and twice as slippery. And your tongue always gets stuck to her.

+++

She's as delicate as a flower—Nothing delicate about that smell, though.

++

As fresh as a daisy—Hey there, Sparky, not for nuthin', but maybe you should get your nose checked out by an ENT . . . real soon.

+++

Curiosity killed the cat—Well, really, what did that cat expect, after waking Curiosity up at that hour of the morning and jumping on the bed, while trying to get under the covers?

++

If a dog is man's best friend—Is a cat man's snotty, passive-aggressive ex-girlfriend?

+++

I'm so hungry, I could eat a horse—Yeah, well, I ate a big breakfast so a pony will be more than enough for me, thank you.

++

It's not the heat it's the humidity—Made all the more unbearably banal by that ridiculous reference to the humidity. And it's still frickin' hot, Swami.

+++

I'm as nervous as a long tailed cat in a living room full of rockers—I'd be nervous too if I was a YouTube video waiting to happen.

++

Any port in any storm—Whatever it takes to shiver me timbers, Matey.

+++

As honest as the day is long—We talkin' regular days or Winter Soltice days?

++

As pure as the driven snow—That big-ass Saint Bernard with the weak bladder has been by here, huh? And what's up with the "driven" stuff? Too lazy to walk?

+++

You can't change a Leopard's spots—Kind of a roundabout way to say that some things are permanent, don't cha think? Maybe you can simplify things a tad . . . that'd be a nice change. Start small maybe?

++

There's more than one way to skin a cat—Really, because why? There's that much cat-skinning going on these days that you need more than one way? What is this, one of those new-fangled arts and crafts classes?

+++

He's a big fish in a small pond—Well, he ain't such a big fish but the smell is certainly on the "big fish" level.

++

She treated me like a dog—Cool . . . fed me, walked me . . . rubbed my belly. Picked up the dump I took on the sidewalk. Kinda cool being her dog. Not liking the leash, though.

+++

He went whole hog—Next time he gets that way, truss him up, throw him on a spit and roast him slowly for a bunch of hours . . . should take him down a peg.

++

Never pet a burning dog—A truism originally uttered by Phil, the one armed, badly charred dog trainer.

+++

Haven't seen that in a coon's age—Hey . . . stop right there . . . not racist . . . it's a raccoon. Really. Look it up.

++

Running dog lackey—Just what the world needs now, a redundant Chinese derivative expression of hate.. because, like most Chinese expressions, we don't have a clue as to what it means. But definitely add "in bed" to the end of it.

+++

Don't be a scaredy-cat—Leave it to you to try to find some benefit to getting the crap scared out of you. No thanks, I'll just wait here.

++

See you later, alligator—That rhyme maybe worked a little when you were four years old, Tupac . . . now it just tells me you're not ready for any kind of poetry slam any time soon.

+++

He's the south end of a north bound horse—Dress it up all you want but, getting to the point, he's still an enormous horse's ass.

++

I quit smoking, cold turkey—Does that make me hungry as a bear, cranky as a mule, and horny as a tomcat? Right, I'm a frickin' zoo. But I really don't miss it in the least . . . uh, mind if I lick your ashtray?

+++

If you can build a better mousetrap—Let's see . . . spring-loaded kill bar, piece of cheese, and . . . well, that's it. What do you want to add, Rube Goldberg, a remote control?

++

What's good for the goose is good for the gander—So, even geese have to deal with breaking the glass ceiling . . . Hard to watch, though. Slender necks and all . . .

+++

Gonna party until the cows come home—Have you ever seen a cow after a debauched night out? Not a pretty sight. Big, red bloodshot hide . . . udder disaster.

++

I want to kill two birds with one stone—Try tying the two of them together with weighted rocks . . . works like a charm every time.

+++

I'm in hog heaven—Maybe, but pretty sure you're gonna wake up in "Ugly as a Pig" hell.

++

Hey, is it hot enough for you?—Usually asked when it's too friggin' hot for anything that doesn't live in the water. No, I'm Beezlebub . . . could use it turned up a few notches.

+++

It's not the heat, it's the humidity—What are you, Al Roker? It's a nasty combination of both . . . made worse by comments like that.

++

Yeah, but it's a dry heat—Here's an idea . . . turn your oven up to 110 and stick your head in there for a few hours. If you're still alive after, I'll agree.

+++

Time will tell—Time will tell nothing . . . if time knows what's good for it . . . or time will be sleeping with the fishes.

++

They say music has the power to soothe the savage beast—yeah, but it won't keep them from tearing you limb from limb . . . soothingly, though.

+++

Great Moments in Clichés - The Arts

"Eighty percent of success is showing up."

–Woody Allen

"Anything worth doing is worth overdoing."

–Mick Jagger

"Dream as if you'll live forever, live as if you'll die today."

–James Dean

"Success is falling nine times and getting up ten."

–Jon Bon Jovi

"We're born alone, we live alone, we die alone. Only through our love and friendship can we create the illusion for the moment that we're not alone."

–Orson Welles

"You know you are getting old when the candles cost more than the cake."

–Bob Hope

"Truth is like the sun. You can shut it out for a time, but it ain't goin' away."

–Elvis Presley

Extra Curricular

"If you want to use a cliché you must take full
responsibility for it yourself and not try to fob it off on
anon., or on society."
—LEWIS THOMAS

"TROUBLE . . . with a capital T . . . that rhymes
with P . . . that stands for . . . persnickety." That's right,
Snarky . . . I changed the lyrics a bit . And?? For the
benefit of this chapter, it made sense . Because these
topics deemed "extracurricular" are clearly those that
can get you into some kind of trouble . . . which starts
with T . . .

"People regurgitate the same old clichés and it becomes like a photocopy of a photocopy of something that's vaguely interesting."
—STEVE COOGAN

Don't be a party pooper

+

Don't be a stick in the mud

+

Trip the light fantastic

+

Clash of the titans

+

Doing something left and right

+

Doing something to beat the band

+

Don't be such a big girl's blouse (English)

+

Earned his wings

+

Fight like a man

+

Fleet footed

+

Good deed for the day

+

He breasted his cards

+

He's a dark horse

+

Might as well, can't dance

+

Winning isn't everything

+

All the world's a stage—I know you THINK that, but half the time, you're playing to the cheap seats and the other half, the audience wants to walk out. Pull the curtain down, will ya?

+++

You can never judge a book by its cover—Right, like anyone cares about books OR their covers anymore. Should be "Never judge a book by how fast it scrolls."

++

You can't judge a book by its cover—Of course you can . . . especially when you put all those unread books on your shelf or coffee table in order to impress your friends.

+++

Caught red-handed—And I knew better . . . should of watched out for those friggin' dye packs.

++

Caught with his hands in the till—Maybe you should have slammed his knuckles in there, over and over again?

+++

Caught with his pants down—All those years his mother warned him about wearing clean underwear and the one time he doesn't listen . . .

++

The check is in the mail—Yep, we all know the rest. The LIES. I kinda like "The check is in my mouth" better . . . much more original.

+++

No use crying over spilled milk—Milk, no . . . but spill a drop of that single malt scotch, now that's another story.

++

He who lives by the sword shall die by the sword—Of course, a machine gun is so much faster and makes a point so much better . . . right, Scarface?

✦✦✦

The pen is mightier than the sword—Not sure who you've been fighting with but I'm not going up against a swordsman with a Paper Mate—not now, not never.

✦✦

Take one for the team—Of course . . . then I can always celebrate from the ER.

✦✦✦

I could do that with one hand tied behind my back— Sure you can, as long as you've got a gun in the other hand.

✦✦

You can bet your bottom dollar—C'mon, use your
pockets . . . or a wallet . . . anywhere else . . . who carries
money there? Disgusting.

+++

We're not in Kansas anymore—No shit, and hard to
believe that there's a place even weirder . . .

++

A rolling stone gathers no moss—Supermodels,
millions of dollars, worldwide acclaim, yes . . . moss, no.

+++

I sleep like a baby—Yeah, well, Percocet and Jameson's
will do that for you.

++

You slept like a baby last night—Does that mean you
pissed yourself and woke up crying?

+++

Don't be an armchair quarterback—Go out there and
get a concussion like a real man.

++

Time to pay the piper—And he's union . . . so it's gonna
cost ya.

+++

Time waits for no man—Now, women on the other
hand? Whole different story. Not only Time but every
man in the vicinity.

++

I'm all thumbs—Bet you have a helluva of a time finding gloves.

✦✦✦

All's well that ends well—Honestly, how often does that happen? Shouldn't we just prepare for "All's shitty that ends shitty" and be happy when we're proven wrong?

✦✦

I have an axe to grind—Hey, you'll find it so much more rewarding when you actually swing it . . . Grinding it is just tedious. Just ask Lizzie Borden.

✦✦✦

The ball is in your court—Right . . . and the judge ain't too happy about it.

✦✦

Been there, seen it, done that—As expected, a
complete waste of time all around.

+++

Blunt words have the sharpest edge—A blunt sword on
the other hand is the sharpest edge you want to have in
any battle.

++

Don't beat yourself up—even though I can see how
incredibly easy, and TEMPTING, it might be to do it.

+++

Don't have a conniption fit—Really? What kind of
fit would you like me to have? And what the hell is a
"conniption" anyway?

++

Fool me once, shame on you, fool me twice, shame on me—Fool me a third time and yes, I am the biggest moron you have ever met.

+++

Good things come to those who wait—Maybe, but better things come to those who pounce immediately.

++

Good things come to those who wait—Hold on . . . it's coming . . . yep, almost there . . . just a few more seconds . . . ah, no, I lied.

+++

He's a bull in a china shop—Which is what Michael Jordan's ex-wife used to say EVERY time they shopped for place settings.

++

He's so artsy-fartsy—Look at you, with your rhymin'
thing. You're a tad artsy-fartsy yourself, ain't ya?

+++

I swear on a stack of Bibles—That's good, because if
you swore off a stack of Bibles, you'd be an atheist. Not
that there's anything wrong with that. Better to swear
on a stack of poker chips.

++

I'd rather have a bottle in front of me than a frontal
lobotomy—Of course, enough bottles and it's
practically the same thing.

+++

Idle hands are the devil's workshop—Boy, you should
see what he can make in that shop . . . no chintzy little
magazine rack for this guy. No sir.

++

It's a blast from the past—Always a crowd-pleaser with the suicide bomber set.

+++

Some days you're the windshield—Other days you're the pedestrian who thought I was gonna stop.

++

Sometimes, you gotta put your foot down—but not when you're doing eighty while texting and eating a sandwich.

+++

This hurts me worse than it does you—Actually, I'm completely fine with the whole thing.

++

This hurts me worse than it does you—Uh, no, scratch that . . . this is definitely gonna hurt you WAY more than it does me.

◆◆◆

This is not my first rodeo—It's my second rodeo . . . so I'm still fairly new at it. By the 3rd or 4th rodeo, I should have it down. Don't rush me.

◆◆

Careful, you'll put your eye out—You hear this so often you'd think we'd be living in a world of one-eyed men.

◆◆◆

You made your bed, now you're gonna have to lie in it— Me, I'd unmake the bed first.

◆◆

Your ass is grass—The classic response . . . I'm the lawn
mower. And welcome to the 3rd grade!

++

You're fishing for compliments—Not me, I usually just
draw a bull's-eye on compliments and blast away with
triple aught buck.

+++

At the drop of a hat—Revise that to "at the drop
of a baseball cap" . . . or maybe even a bandana.
Welcome to this century. Hats? No so much anymore.
Thankfully.

++

You're banging your head against a brick wall—Nice
job, Sherlock . . . can you tell by all the red dust on my
forehead or by the weird indentations?

+++

One size fits all—No such thing. It's either too tight or you're swimming in it. Next time, use a mirror.

++

I'm not just whistling Dixie—Well, that's good. The war's been over for 150 years . . . in most states.

+++

Let's bat that idea around—Here's an even better idea . . . how about we put in a designated hitter?

++

Life's too short—Right. Really very sorry, Life, for all those dashed NBA dreams.

+++

BEST ✦ MELLOW OUT ✦ HOLD A CANDLE TO ✦ PIPE

We'll jump that fence when we get to it—**You do realize that jumping fences before you get to them leaves really nasty bruises, yes?**

++

The eyes are the mirrors (windows) of (to) the soul—**Word of advice . . . keep those Ray-Bans on.**

+++

A baptism of fire—**I think I like the 'hold your head/ dunk it in the water' thing a LOT better.**

++

You're asking for Trouble with a capital "T"—**which rhymes with "P," which stands for "You're a Poor excuse for a Human Being."**

+++

I've got high hopes—Yeah, me too . . . that I can drive this car at 115 mph while eating a pizza and taking hits off a bong without attracting any unwanted attention.

◆◆

Maybe something will jog his memory—The only thing that will "jog" his memory is a Louisville Slugger to the side of the head. What's that? Something's coming back to you?

◆◆◆

The Most Hated Clichés

"At the end of the day" (Also known as "When all is said and done")—THE fall back cliché for the manager/leader who has no idea what to do or how to do it, but has been given the task of getting it done. Used as a "summing up", it can be more irritating than fingernails on a chalkboard (also a cliché).

"It's not rocket science"—Used to verbally demonstrate how easy something should be, once again by people who wouldn't know how to do the thing with 12 years of education and a refresher course minutes before the project was undertaken.

"Basically" or "literally"—Used as a stall for time by those who don't have the wherewithal to think fast on their feet but don't want to sound like a complete dolt through peppering their speech with "likes" and "you knows."

"To be fair"—That is, without fail, almost always followed by a statement that is not only completely biased but inevitably, grossly unfair.

"Going forward"—A highly regarded preface to any sentence because it's a clear demarcation that we will no longer be going backwards.

"To be honest"—Clearly, you've been lying to me from the jump and are only now going to 'fess up. Or are you?

"let's face it"—Because, after all, I've had my backside to it the entire time.

"In the pipeline"—And much like any large pipeline I've ever come into contact with, there's a stench surrounding it that could remove paint.

"Touch base"—Meaning "Talk to me later" . . . or, more to the point, that I should track you down and present a case for a solution to a problem that you couldn't possibly figure out but will happily take credit for fixing in the end. Or should I say, at the end of the day.

Politics and the Media

"I think my whole generation's mission is to kill
the cliché."
—BECK

THERE IS NO ONE place where the cliché runs
as wild and free as much as it does in the media. Books,
music, television, newspapers, radio . . . go more than
10 minutes without hearing one and you've stumbled
onto an alternate universe where things can only be
better. But be careful . . . it's a long and winding road;
fraught with the perils that is mankind.*

*TAIC (They're everywhere!)

"In every election in American history both parties have their clichés. The party that has the clichés that ring true wins."
—NEWT GINGRICH

Yellow journalism

Media circus

The liberal media

Sounding off

It sparked a controversy

Case in point

Don't want to cover old ground

Emergency situation

Epidemic proportions

You field this one

Firestorm/storm of protest/ controversy

Go by the book

He's a fall guy

Heated debate

He's an easy study

He's so matter-of-fact

A hidden agenda

I didn't expect the Spanish Inquisition

I got hosed

Mixed reviews

Nice play, Shakespeare.

Web of intrigue

Tarred and feathered

That's skull duggery

Watch your tongue

An old blowhard

Sworn affidavit

State-of-the- art

A watched pot never boils—but is clearly much more interesting than pretty much anything on network TV . . . and most of cable.

◆◆◆

She's got a bee in her bonnet—I'm going down to see Andy and Opie at the Sheriff's office . . . and bringing Barney his bullet. Left it on the credenza at my house, of all places.

◆◆

I'm caught between a rock and a hard place— Getting this whole *127 Hours* visual of cutting my arm off with a pen knife.

◆◆◆

I'm free as a bird—Yeah, well, crap on my windshield just once and you'll see why the caged bird sings.

◆◆

Great Moments in Clichés - Presidents

"That government is best which governs the least, because its people discipline themselves."

—Thomas Jefferson

"All right" or "O.K."

—Martin Van Buren

"With me it is exceptionally true that the Presidency is no bed of roses."

—James K. Polk (originated in a Christopher Marlowe poem, but not in the vain we use most today)

"Good ballplayers make good citizens."

—Chester A. Arthur

"Speak softly and carry a big stick."

—Theodore Roosevelt

For Pete's sake—Ok, I'll do it for God. I'll do it for country . . . but who the hell is Pete?

+++

It's the real thing—Man, is there anything as trite as quoting a soft drink commercial? What's next, you want to teach the world to sing?

+++

It paled in comparison—Paled? It makes David Bowie look like George Hamilton.

++

I'm ready for booze and broads—Relax, Sinatra. It'll be closing time real soon.

+++

I'm his number one fan—That got to be a really creepy cliché after Stephen King's *Misery*.

++

Great Moments in Clichés - Presidents Redux

You can fool all of the people some of the time, and some of the people all of the time, but you can not fool all of the people all of the time."

–Abraham Lincoln*

"Do I not destroy my enemies when I make them my friends?"

–Abraham Lincoln

"Above all, tell the truth."

–Grover Cleveland

"A man is known by the company he keeps, and also by the company from which he is kept out."

–Grover Cleveland

"And so my fellow Americans, ask not what your country can do for you; ask what you can do for your country."

–John F. Kennedy

---

* Before the whole Zombie/Vampire thing.

Cliché Hall of Famer #1 - Ben Franklin*, Part Deux

"Axe to grind"

"Speak ill of no man, but speak all the good you know of everybody."

"It takes many good deeds to build a good reputation, and only one bad one to lose it."

"In this world nothing can be said to be certain, except death and taxes." (Could also be credited to Daniel Defoe).

"Applause waits on success."
"Believe none of what you hear and half of what you see."

Yes, this is a short chapter . . . but *The Snark Handbook: Politics & Government Edition* is out, and I'm killing two birds with one stone.

*Yep, definitely too much electricity. Definitely. What am I, Rain Man?

Money

"It's the age-old thing - it's such a cliché - but why worry about things you have no control over?"
—MIKE QUADE

"MONEY MAKES THE WORLD go 'round" .
. . . "Money is the root of all evil" . . . . "Money can't buy you happiness" . . .
The almighty dollar. Going for the gold.
See . . . almost a Herculean task to talk about any of these subjects and <u>NOT</u> fall back on the multitude of inane and banal clichés that have passed for wisdom oh, these many years. It's enough to make you see green.

"Too many people spend money they haven't earned, to buy things they don't want, to impress people they don't like."

—WILL ROGERS*

Even money	Feather your nest	The fickle finger of fate
Filthy rich	High and the mighty (the)	Final analysis
Highway robbery	Kick butt	Get the sack
A wheeler dealer	Cut a fine figure	Gird your loins
I want my place in the sun	Don't use a lot where a little will do	Head honcho
	Down the drain/toilet	He's a bald faced liar
		Reign supreme
		Went belly up

*Yeah, I know, it's not about clichés, but I liked it and wanted to use it. So deal with it.

Two wrongs don't make a right—But three wrongs and they make it a law.

+++

The butler did it—Easy to blame the manservants . . . . They don't have a union, a lawyer, or anything—talk about bad PR. This whole *Downton Abbey* thing is out of hand.

++

All talk and no action—Really? Apply for a gig in the U.S. Congress. No experience necessary.

+++

I'm as busy as a one-legged man in an ass kickin' contest—Just pause for a moment and visualize this. Kinda fun, eh? Hey, do they really have "ass-kicking contests?" Where do you sign up?

++

All that glitters is not gold—but none of the rest really matters.

+++

All work and no play makes Jack a dull boy—Of course the same can be said for Bill (Gates), Donald (Trump) and Warren (Buffet)—they all managed "dull" pretty well.

++

And you can take that to the bank—but they're gonna need real money if you want that toaster.

+++

As poor as dirt—Of course, how poor would you be if that dirt was undeveloped land in Manhattan (if there was any) that would sell for $2,500 a square foot. Not so dirty anymore . . .

++

At the bottom of the pecking order—Still leaves you with some pretty nasty scars.

+++

At the end of the day—Why do we always have to wait until the end of the day? Can't we make a decision now? Is something going to be different then? No. So, I say, let's vote now.

++

Beggars can't be choosers—Sure they can, they really have nothing to lose so why not be a little choosy?

+++

Better late than never—You know, that never seems to work. They always seem to want you here on time. Go figure.

++

He was born with a silver spoon in his mouth—His mother was not happy about it . . . she couldn't walk for days afterwards.

+++

She's sleeping her way to the top—Yessir, you talk about your school of hard knocks . . . and nothing but A+ in every class.

++

A penny saved is a penny earned—Just ninety-nine more and you can get a lottery ticket. And then start throwing all those pennies back into the jar again.

+++

Give a man a fish and he'll eat for a day; teach a man to fish and he'll eat for a lifetime—but guaranteed, he'll get tired of fish by day three or four. Then he'll be back to being pissing and moaning.

++

He's had a checkered career—Without the strategic
significance a "chess" ered career might have provided.

✦✦✦

Art imitates life—So that's why my life keeps coming
up like an empty soup can.

✦✦

Opportunity doesn't knock twice—Most times it just
passes right over to the next house. All I get is those
Watchtower folks.

✦✦✦

Early to bed, early to rise, makes a man healthy,
wealthy and wise—and boring as shit.

✦✦

If a tree falls in the forest, does it make a sound?—Or if I write a snark and nobody reads it, will I get paid? Sorry, got to bring it home.

+++

It cost me an arm and a leg—but you should see the savings I get on a pair of shoes.

++

Rising tide lifts all boats—Funny how they always leave out the part about how only the filthy rich can actually afford any kind of a boat these days.

+++

Too many Indians, not enough Chiefs—Really? In the PC world we live in, that's the cliché you choose? In fact, it's the other way around—too many middle managers trying to prove that their jobs have some meaning and nobody actually doing the work.

++

It's all in a day's work—Interesting. I'm surprised you
know that one as you've never actually "worked" a day
in your life.

+++

Success has a thousand fathers while failure is an
orphan—but failure still collects those child support
payments every month so who's the real success here?

++

I've got to tackle my homework—Why? Talk about a
senseless, pointless hit.

+++

'Armed to the teeth—which is only cool if you're facing
an army of dentists.

++

What's the bottom line?—The bottom line is the demarcation mark for where you should be inserting your head.

+++

We're going to burn the midnight oil—It's over there on the shelf next to the daybreak oil, the noontime oil and the why the hell do I need so many different kinds of "oil" oil.

++

I'll be laughing all the way to the bank—At which point they will start laughing at me the entire time I'm meeting with their loan officers. It'll start as soon as I pull out my tax returns.

+++

Calls it quits—The rest of us called it being fired.

++

While the tailor rests, the needle rusts—That's because
the factory is a non-air conditioned, non-union,
sweat shop.

+++

Red sky in the morning, sailor's warning; red sky at
night, sailor's delight—It takes so little to keep sailors
happy.

++

Too many cooks in the kitchen—The INS can fix that
in no time.

+++

Oh well, another day, another dollar—And I went to
college for this.

++

I'm low man on the totem pole—which pretty much puts my head directly up someone else's ass.

+++

Hammer out an agreement—and it's going to be hammered against your head. I think we'll agree.

++

Pinko—Used to be a communist sympathizer, today it describes half of the Democrat politicians. Or really cute sweatpants.

+++

General consensus—Meaning it involves good intentions, a desire to compromise, and the ability to have non-personality driven communication— obviously, an archaic expression today.

++

It's harder for a rich man to go to heaven than for a camel to go through the eye of a needle—The only teaching from the Bible that's completely ignored by Republicans.

+++

They took me to the cleaners—Yeah, but there's no chance they'll be able to get those stains out. They're there for life.

++

Business Clichés

Core Competency—Fundamental strength, although one would think you'd want someone to shoot a tad higher than just "competent".

Buy-In—Agreement on a course of action. Can't just believe, gotta cost ya some jing to boot. Used to a much more useful effect in poker.

Empower—Give added responsibilities to those below you. Can there be anything more condescending? Who are you, the Burger King?

Corporate Values—Corporations are people now? Nope. Soylent green is people, tho.

Make Hay—Be productive or successful quickly. Also used with "while the sun shines" because after the sun goes down, you're going to need to get as soused as you possibly can from all that hay making.

Think Outside the Box—To approach a problem in an unusual way, or using a different method. Overused 101. Every time I hear it, it conjures up those Russian nesting dolls and visions of the speaker stuck inside so many boxes that no one could possibly hear him/her scream.

Leverage—To manipulate or control. As in, to leverage your standing in the community to take unfair advantage over those lesser peons out there.

Vertical—A specific area of expertise. Would really prefer it if you were horizontal, face on the ground.

Learnings—Bizarre conjugations now pass for "expertise". Take the English Language and make it your own. No one will notice.

Boil the Ocean—Waste time. If only you could, we could make the world's largest pot of Moron Soup.

Reach Out—Set up a meeting. I hear that and I want to do a Four Tops pirouette and chime in with "I'll be there".

Punt—Give up an idea. Also used with "drop back six" . . . Usually said by someone who has blocked more than their share of punts in their day . . . and usually with their face.

Impact—The difference between "affect" and "effect". Your phony affect has had an effect on me—I want to puke.

Give 110%—Can't be done, Sparky. Might be time for that refresher math class . . . from the 3rd grade.

Take It To The Next Level—make something better. Cool. When you look into your crystal ball and glimpse what that "next level" might be, call me. I'll come a-runnin'.

It Is What It Is—And the World Champion belt and undisputed King of The Obvious crown goes to . . .

Friends and Family

"A friend is one who knows you and loves you just the same."
—ELBERT HUBBARD

IN MUCH THE SAME way that the chapter on the opposite sex examined a world rife with pitfalls and dangers, so does this particular section . . . because when you get down to the interaction with <u>other people</u>, the same thing almost inevitably happens . . . all hell breaks loose.
Take a look.

"Distant relatives are the best kind . . . the further the better."
—KIN HUBBARD

Banding together to beat the odds

✦

What's a little

_____

amongst friends

✦

Under the same roof

✦

Some of my best friends

✦

Traditional family values

✦

Creature comforts

✦

A guiding light

✦

A winning combination

✦

Everyman

✦

Hold down the fort

✦

Women and children first!

✦

Welcome to . . .

✦

What began as . . . turned into . . .

✦

They are (he/she is) not alone.

✦

School's out

✦

Yes, DO throw out the baby with the bath water.
Start over.

+++

Children should be seen and not heard—Have you
seen what some of these kids are wearing. I'll pass on
the seeing if you don't mind.

++

Chip off the old block—and still dumber than a rock.

+++

Am I my brother's keeper?—Only if you're planning on
making a grab for dad's fortune.

++

You can pick your friends—and you can pick your nose, but you can't pick your friend's nose. Well, you can . . . but then it really starts to get weird.

+++

Any friend of his is a friend of mine—This is the friend that likes to lend people money, right?

++

All for one and one for all—Then why did D'Artagnan get all that attention?

+++

Good fences make good neighbors—and keeps their dog off of your lawn. Just don't get caught "borrowing a cup of sugar" (wink, wink) from the comely missus of the house.

++

If you don't have anything nice to say, don't say anything at all—We need to revise this to say don't text anything either.

+++

Lit up like a Christmas tree—Christmas is just a funner holiday. Nobody EVER says "Lit up like a Menorah" . . . besides not casting enough light, it just boring as all get out.

++

He's airing his dirty laundry—glad we live upwind.

+++

It's like my daddy used to say—You mean, other than "Don't make me get up or else . . . shut up and go to bed . . . I'll give you something to cry about . . . Shut up and deal?"

++

Every parent's worst nightmare—They never have a clue. Their worst nightmare is not even close to how bad it could be.

+++

Spare the rod, spoil the child—Use the rod, get six months probation and you're visiting your child under strict supervision.

++

You're the gleam in your father's eye—and the drain on his wallet, his love life, his sanity, but hey, don't let go of that gleam.

+++

Ah, to be young and foolish—but more importantly, to be young.

++

Young, dumb and full of—uh . . . rum? It used to be piss and vinegar. The youth of today have it so much easier . . . and much, much sexier.

+++

Early to bed, early to rise makes a man—a well-rested boring old fart that's up way too early for his or anyone's own good.

++

Far be it from me—which is exactly where I'd like to be, far be it from you.

+++

He couldn't hit the broad side of a barn—but I'll happily drive him out to the country, find a barn, and see for myself . . . but I'm leaving him there.

++

Let's cross that bridge when we come to it—Well, when, and IF (Big IF), we come to that bridge, one of us is going over the side of that bridge (two guesses who, and the first is a gimme).

✦✦✦

Pot calling the kettle black—but not to his face, of course.

✦✦

So much bad in the best of us and so much good in the worst in us—that it ill-behoves us to talk about the rest of us.

✦✦✦

Stand pat—Actually, I can't stand Pat. In fact, I can't stand a single one of those Irish bastids.

✦✦

Blow this pop stand—Hey, don't leave Mom out of this equation.

+++

You can't blame me for trying—No, but for failing, all kinds of blame. You betcha.

++

Big brother is watching—Just like he used to do when you showered.

+++

Dutch uncle—leave it to the Dutch. They sure know how to make friends and be diplomatic. You keep that finger in the dike, Hans, and the family reunion will go so much smoother.

++

There are starving children in Africa—It costs over $200 to ship to Africa, so go ahead, take my broccoli and mail it there.

+++

Fake it till you make it—The motto for an entire generation. Learn something? Nah, not interested.

++

Motherhood and apple pie—It's getting harder and harder to find authentic versions of either.

+++

Great Moments in Clichés – Presidents Redux

"A man who has never lost himself in a cause bigger than himself has missed one of life's mountaintop experiences. Only in losing himself does he find himself."

–Richard Nixon

"The time comes upon every public man when it is best for him to keep his lips closed."

–Abraham Lincoln

"Read my lips. No new taxes."

–George H.W. Bush

"The ballot is stronger than the bullet."

–Abraham Lincoln

"I did not have sexual relations with that woman."

–Bill Clinton

"If I had eight hours to chop down a tree, I'd spend six hours sharpening my ax"

–Abraham Lincoln*

"If you can't convince them, confuse them."

–Harry S. Truman

"A friend is one who has the same enemies as you have"

–Abraham Lincoln

* I'm thinking "work smarter not harder"

Food

"Civilization as it is known today could not have evolved, nor can it survive, without an adequate food supply."
—NORMAN BORLAUG

. . . BUT ONLY IF WE had stopped at "adequate". Today, we as a people are walking clichés . . . and one could argue that food is the mother lode source of that cliché-ness (??). "We are what we eat" . . . well, then we're a society of junk food and crap. And wherever junk and crap go, the cliché is almost certainly sure to follow.

"They might be dirty, and cheap, and their food might taste like shit, but at least they didn't speak in clichés."
—NEIL GAIMAN

Eat humble pie

Few fries short of a happy meal

He's a bubble shy of plumb

Feast your eyes on this

Cut and dried

He's a corn-fed hick

Few sandwiches short of a picnic

Fat slob

He's an inch deep and a mile wide

Get stuffed

Eat dirt

He's milktoast

Half seas over

Enough already

Wash your mouth out with soap

Hair of the dog

Full of himself

Best thing since little green apples—Fast cars, cable TV, 3D movies—ok maybe. Little green apples? Bar's pretty low. Same goes for sliced bread.

+++

Carrot on a stick—And that will make me chase after it, why?

++

Life is a bowl of cherries—Screw that, life should really be a bowl of Xanax.

+++

An apple a day keeps the doctor away—Mostly because no HMO in America covers fruit of any variety.

++

As slow as molasses—because we measure speed by the flow of a viscous, mashed sugar cane substance. As fast as high fructose corn syrup? Doesn't seem to work.

+++

Butter wouldn't melt in her mouth—or anywhere else, for that matter, but how much fun would it be to try it? Cue *Last Tango*.

++

Don't put all your eggs in one basket—After a while, it's just a basket full of old, rotten eggs.

+++

Got your hand caught in the cookie jar—Serves you right for having a snapping lid on your cookie jar.

++

I'm gonna look out for number one—**You definitely should, after eating that Super Grande Burrito Especiale platter you had last night. The rest of us will be looking out for number two.**

+++

It's hard to make lemonade—**when life just keeps whipping lemons at your face.**

++

Red sky at night, eat a cupcake—**Red sky in the morning, eat another cupcake.**

+++

Wake up and smell the coffee—**What's that? You're single and didn't make coffee. Run!**

++

You are what you eat—So you're telling me I'm a giant
Hostess cupcake, a bag of Cheetos, and a foot-long
Subway sandwich?

+++

You say potato, I say potahto—who are you kidding?
Nobody says potahto.

++

If I'd known you were coming—I'd have baked a
MUCH bigger cake.

+++

He knows which side his bread is buttered on—and
yet, at the end of the day, he still has a handful of
butter.

++

Life is like a box of chocolates, you never know
what you are going to get—but guaranteed, there's a
toothache involved.

+++

Goes against the grain—First lactose, then wheat, now
grain? What are you, Felix Unger?

++

An ounce of prevention is worth a pound of cure—but
a pound of cured bacon is worth a lifetime.

+++

Bringing home the bacon—Don't stop there. Bring
home the eggs, home fries, toast, and coffee, too.

++

Where's the beef?—Hey, this is a fast food restaurant, there ain't no beef, only "beef products."

+++

Everything in moderation—Especially the need to say "Everything in moderation."

++

That and a quarter will get you a cup of coffee—Of course today, "that" equals $5.00. Brother, can you spare your Amex card for a cup of Joe.

+++

Great Moments in Clichés – Authors Redux

"A rose by any other name would smell as sweet"
                                              –William Shakespeare

"Don't throw the baby out with the bath water."
                                              –Thomas Murner (loosely credited)

"Bated breath"
                                              –Shakespeare

Best of both worlds "If this is best of possible worlds . . . all is for the best"
                                              –Voltaire

"The optimist proclaims that we live in the best of all possible worlds; and the pessimist fears this is true"
                                              –James Branch Cable

"Takes the biscuit / Takes the cake"
  –James Joyce (in *Dubliners*, 1914, but could have appeared in Latin as early as 1610)

"You can't have your cake and eat it too"
                                              –John Heywood

"Catch-22"
                                              –Joseph Heller

"A chip off the old block"
  –Theocrites, "*A chip of the old flint*" from the poem 'Idylls'

"Cut the mustard"
                                              –O Henry

The Good Life

"Oh, the good life, full of fun . . . ."
—TONY BENNETT

THINK WHEN TONY BENNETT sang
those lyrics, he was referring to the banal cliché the
phrase has come to mean? What exactly is "the good
life?" Booze, broads, and blow? Great music, fine food,
a fabulous vista from a posh hotel? Who knows. What
I do know is that it ain't so good anymore . . . so snark
them bad boys!

"Travel is only glamorous in retrospect"
—PAUL THEROUX

Cheap knock-off

Wait-and-see attitude

Half seas over

Carrying coal to Newcastle

While away the hours

I busted my hump

Chuck-a-nana: throwing a temper tantrum (Australia)

Step up

Mellow out

Thin as six o'clock

Crisis proportions

There for the taking

Twice as nice

This point in time

Fun and games

That's as American as apple pie—Seems about right, today apple pie, tomorrow stale, hard crust filled with rancid fruit.

+++

All roads lead to Rome—which leads to one hell of a traffic jam.

++

As solid as the ground we stand on—Obviously never lived in Malibu.

+++

Be it ever so humble there's no place like home—And why do we think that's a good thing? After all when was the last time you entered "humble" in your vacation search parameters.

++

A Journey of a thousand miles begins with one step—
Or . . . you could just fly . . . or take the train . . . a bus,
a bus is good. Cars . . . cars would work.

+++

When in Rome, do as the Romans do—Basically make
fun of the Americans and try to rip them off selling
them cheap shit.

++

In a New York minute—which we all know is about
forty seconds

+++

Ten foot pole—would have put Poland in the running
at the Olympic High Jump Competition

++

I'm going to tie one on—From the looks of things, you couldn't tie your shoes let alone "one on." How about we concentrate on getting from the bar to the car?

+++

I don't give a fig—From the expression on your face, it's look like you don't give much of anything. Try prunes next time.

+++

Home is where the heart is—When considering any organ any farther south, a hotel is a much better choice.

++

I need to sow my wild oats—Well, let's just hope the ground isn't overly fertile or your planting days will be over quickly.

+++

He couldn't get to first base—**Great, more Baseball
imagery . . . I'm really more of a soccer fan . . .
GOOAALLL!**

◆◆

My cup runneth over—**Well, maybe you should stop
at one.**

◆◆◆

I'm going to drown my sorrows—**You do that. Drown
'em real good . . . and then vomit up all your regrets.
You'll feel better . . . and thank me. You watch and see.**

◆◆

Short pleasures are often long regretted—**but oh, can
they bring a smile to your face.**

◆◆◆

Great Moments in Clichés - The Arts Redux

"In order to succeed, your desire for success should be greater than your fear of failure."

–Bill Cosby

"Just cause you got the monkey off your back doesn't mean the circus has left town."

–George Carlin

"You always pass failure on the way to success."

–Mickey Rooney

"You've achieved success in your field when you don't know whether what you're doing is work or play"

–Warren Beatty

"Behind every successful man is a woman, behind her is his wife."

–Groucho Marx

"I've had a wonderful time, but this wasn't it"

–Groucho Marx

"Cried all the way to the bank"

–Liberace

You need some hair of the dog that bit you—Bad enough we have to deal with a throbbing headache and a mouth that tastes like old socks, do we really have to suck back a cure called "hair of the dog?" Pretty cruel and unusual.

++

It's my ace in the hole—Damn, don't even want to think about the King or the Queen . . . or how you're going to get them on the table.

+++

I've got an ace up my sleeve—Note to self: Never play poker with this guy, especially when he's wearing a long sleeve shirt.

++

I would bet the farm—Go ahead . . . but remember: Caesar's Palace? Largest farm owners in America. Even have a bunch of fake farms from Facebook that people lost.

+++

It's not whether you win or lose, it's how you play the game—Nope . . . it's definitely about winning. Sorry, Charlie.

✦✦

Let the chips fall where they may—The perfect thing to say right before you flip over the poker table.

✦✦✦

He's not playing with a full deck—Looks more like he's holding a hand full of jokers. You are what you bet.

✦✦

If you play your cards right—Let's just say that, if you don't, there's this guy named Carmine who will be giving you a call.

✦✦✦

All bets are off—Sure, now that I'm winning . . . gonna
stop the free drinks, too?

✦✦

Lady Luck was smiling on me—Lady Luck wouldn't
know you if there were a neon sign flashing "You" every
five seconds.

✦✦✦

You win some you lose some—You just go on believing
that, Slim . . . the house odds keep getting better every
time you play.

✦✦

If you're gonna blow smoke up my ass—please do it
while you're getting high. My ass loves that shit.

✦✦✦

She'll be seeing pink elephants—Oh right, because
seeing a grey elephant in this bar wasn't strange enough
to describe being shitfaced?

✦✦

Aren't you on the wagon?—Yes sir . . . and I'm riding it straight to a bar.

+++

Hit it right on the nose—I'll let it go this time but next time, keep the rest of your face out of my coke, okay? Use the dollar bill I gave ya.

++

Put that in your pipe and smoke it—I'll put it in my pipe but I'm also ready to flush it down the crapper at the first sign of the cops.

+++

Unlucky at cards, lucky in love—Either way, you're gonna lose your shirt.

++

I'm in dire straits—Oh yeah? Big fan of "Money for Nothing" and "Brothers in Arms" . . . and don't forget, the chicks are free.

+++

Miscellany

"You need clichés. Clichés are what people respond to."
—MATTHEW VAUGHN

AS WITH MANY OF the previous books, there
are a number of quotes and/or snarks that defy catego-
rization, that live "outside the box" and "march to a
different drummer." This is that catch-all chapter for
those clichés. What's that you say . . . "Hey, Mr. Snark,
sounds like you're as lazy as the day is long!" Well,
yeah . . .

TAKE   ◆   WHAT'S A LITTLE _____ AMONG FRIENDS   ◆   TARRED

"Show me a man with both feet on the ground, and I'll show you a man who can't put his pants on."
—JOE E. LEWIS

Welcome to the club	Tense standoff	Place was crawling with cops
A closed mouth gathers no feet	Execution-style	Cult of personality
Store bought	He's all hat and no cattle	Try your hand at something
What in tarnation?	Very real concern	Full Monty
To be honest with you	A few sandwiches short of a picnic	Roost

In the kingdom of the blind, the one-eyed man pretends to be blind—because nobody really wants to stand out like that, right?

+++

Neither hide nor hair—I haven't seen her/him but if I see any part of him, hair included, I'll be sure to hide.

++

Six of one and half a dozen of another—Why can't you just say twelve? Just say that, okay? We gotta do math now?

+++

Busy hands are happy hands—and idle hands will put a smile on your face.

++

ROBBERY ✦ GET STUFFED ✦ TAKE OFF, YOU HOSER,

Make tracks—What am I now, Tonto?

+++

She uses more clichés than you can shake a stick at—If she uses another one, maybe we shake the stick at her head.

++

It's as good as new—Who are you kidding? It's never as good as new, and anything you touch usually falls apart in your hands.

+++

It's all very cutting edge—and tomorrow it'll be as dull as a blunt ax.

++

You know what they say—Nobody knows what "they" say, no one knows what you say, and you know I never will.

✦✦✦

As luck would have it—Luck saw this from the jump and ran in the opposite direction.

✦✦

Evolutionary not Revolutionary—We get it, you're talking about incremental change. But the fact that this rhymes does not merit that ridiculously smug look you get after you say it.

✦✦✦

There now, that wasn't so bad, was it?—The thing is, it always is.

✦✦

We need to blaze a new trail—but given the level of your abilities, the only thing that'll happen is you'll burn the house down.

+++

He's always stepping on people's toes—You can't blame him . . . he's just trying to get a higher view.

++

Rules are made to be broken—and I'm doing my best to keep people from being disappointed.

+++

Ignorance is bliss—and can occasionally make for a great alibi.

++

By all means, after you—just don't forget I let you go first. Like I'm gonna let you forget.

+++

It was a wakeup call—Right . . . for now . . . but, trust me, next week it will be back to business as usual.

++

She's so artsy-craftsy—the PC version of artsy-fartsy.

+++

Smart ass—They always center on that part of the anatomy . . . not "smart brain" or "smart heart". . . kinda makes you wonder, no?

++

Hit the road—be careful . . . when the road hits back, it can be quite messy and often fatal.

+++

I beg to differ—hey, I'll beg for a lot of things but differing . . . not a chance.

++

What's cookin' good lookin'?—Say that and then leave that person alone with the food in the kitchen? Yeah, I think I'll pass.

+++

What's not to like?—Welllll . . . how much time do you have?

++

Experts agree—Uh huh. Never happens. It's like one size fits all.

+++

Is the glass half-empty or half-full?—Doesn't matter ... it spilled red wine all over a white tablecloth, staining everything.

++

Imitation is the sincerest form of flattery—Sure, sidesteps all the plagiarism issues.

+++

History repeats itself—It just keeps giving us chances to do it right. How come we never take them?

++

To the best of my knowledge—which, come to think of it, is not worth a whole lot.

+++

Laughter is the best medicine—and that's about all that's covered by my HMO's medical insurance.

++

Watching the clock—Tick, tick, tick. I really need a hobby. Or something . . . work? Nah.

+++

Kit and caboodle—Research shows it was originally "kit and boodle" but that sounded too much like the next guest of the *Ed Sullivan Show* (right after the dancing bears who can spin plates . . . oh, yeah and the Beatles).

++

The End

almost ...

Conclusion

WELL, THAT'S IT, FELLOW linguistic snobs. We have come to the end of our tether. The party's over. We have grabbed the bull by the horns and took the reins. Easy as pie, no?

What's that you say? It's not the end of the world? Why can't we use a cliché every now and again?

Well . . .

If it were only as sporadic as that . . . if only it WAS "now and then" . . . but it ain't. People use cliché's more than Carter's got liver pills . . . more than you can shake a stick at . . .

So you're shit out of luck . . . caught between a rock and a hard place . . . up a creek without a paddle . . .

(My lord, won't somebody PLEASE stop this? Who's got the bullets? I'm buyin'!)

And remember . . . At the end of the day, when all is said and done, it ain't over until the fat lady sings.

It is what it is.

AS ALWAYS, I OWE an attitude of gratitude (cliché) to the following:

James Naccarato—Who I couldn't have done it without (cliché)

Mark Mirando—Who was always there for me (cliché)

Mom—(Just mentioning her is one of the major clichés)

And, true to form (cliché), the light of my life (cliché), and the one who gives it all meaning (sigh—enough already?) . . . Rosalind.

*Clichés That Should Have Made This Book:**

_____

_____

_____

_____

_____

_____

_____

_____

_____

_____

_____

_____

_____

_____

_____

_____

_____

_____

_____

*And no, you're not getting any royalties.

Clichés That Shouldn't Have Made This Book:*

_____

_____

_____

_____

_____

_____

_____

_____

_____

_____

_____

_____

_____

_____

_____

_____

_____

_____

_____

_____

_____

*Like I really care what you think . . .